Keeping a Corn

GW00992447

by
Michael J. McEachern

Table of Contents

Introduction 2

General Information 3

Choosing a Corn Snake 8

Housing and Maintenance 15

Feeding and Growth of Corn Snakes 22

Winter Cooling of Adult Corn Snakes.......................28

Feeding and Growth Patterns of Hibernated Adults.........31

Breeding and Egg Laying...................................35

Skin Shedding 50

Diseases and Disorders.....................................54

Introduction

Why Keep a Corn Snake?

The corn snake, *Elaphe guttata*, was one of the first species of snake to be regularly raised and bred in captivity. The ease with which it can be kept combined with its attractive and varied colors have made it a favorite of snake keepers both in the U.S. and in Europe. The popularity of corn snakes can be attributed to the following:

Attractive Appearance. Most people consider the corn snake to be one of the more attractively colored and patterned species of snake. In addition, there is considerable variety in the color, and, to a lesser extent, in the markings of corn snakes, due both to selectively bred mutations and to natural variation. One could keep a dozen corn snakes with no two looking alike.

Good Temperament. The disposition of individual adult corn snakes can range from fair to excellent, with very good to excellent being the norm. Babies and wild caught animals may bite, but time in captivity will almost always eliminate this.

Ease of Keeping. Corn snakes score well here too. They typically feed well in captivity and eat food items (mice) that are easy to obtain. They are not unduly prone to illness. They reproduce readily in captivity. The moderate size of adult corn snakes makes them large enough to suit most people's tastes without being cumbersome to house or potentially hazardous to the keeper. Additionally, more is known about keeping corn snakes in captivity than is known for most other snakes. Awareness of this information helps prevent mistakes that others have previously made.

Ready Availability. The great numbers of corn snakes bred in captivity have helped to make baby corn snakes widely available at reasonable prices. Adults, both wild-caught and captive-raised, are also often available.

In short, the corn snake is an ideal animal for a person without previous experience at keeping snakes yet it can remain a favorite of people with experience at keeping many kinds of snakes.

General Information

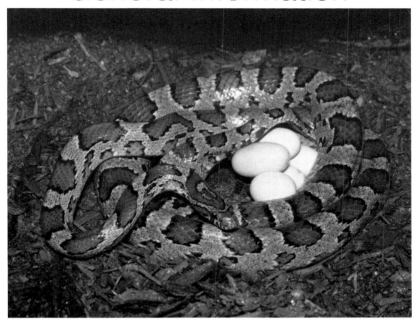

A female corn snake *(Elaphe guttata guttata)* in the process of laying eggs.

Origin of the Name

The name corn snake is derived from the corn fields and corncribs where early Americans would sometimes encounter this snake when the animal was hunting for mice or other small rodents. The scientific name for the corn snake, *Elaphe guttata*, is derived from the Greek word 'elaphe' meaning deerskin and the Latin word 'guttatus' meaning spotted or speckled. Corn snakes are certainly spotted, with large and prominent blotches that run down their backs, and their skin, with its smooth or weakly keeled scales, does indeed have the feel of fine soft leather. Another common name that is sometimes used for the corn snake is 'red rat snake'. This name is derived from the red-orange color of many corn snakes, and the fact that members of the genus *Elaphe* are collectively referred to as rat snakes because of their food preferences.

Size, Markings, and Characteristics

Hatchling corn snakes are 9-14 inches (23-36 cm) in total length. Adults are generally two and a half to five feet (76-152 cm) with the record being six feet (183 cm). Males more readily achieve larger sizes.

Corn snakes are characterized by a series of blotches, often outlined in black, that run down the back of the animal. Additional smaller blotches often are present on the sides. The first blotch on the back of the neck splits to form two stripes that run on top of the head and meet to form a characteristic spearpoint. Additional stripes run along the sides of the head, through the eyes and meet on top of the head in front of the eyes. The ground color varies between orange, grey and brown and the blotches are typically either darker or more red than the ground color. A faint pair of dark stripes sometimes runs through the dorsal blotches. Baby corn snakes typically display more contrast and less orange pigmentation in their markings than do adults. The bellies of most corn snakes are usually marked with bold black checks on a white or orange background. The ventral checks, which can sometimes be mostly orange or largely absent, fuse into stripes on the underside of the tail. Scales are present in 25-35 rows at midbody. The anal plate is divided into two scales.

Subspecies

Two, or sometimes three, subspecies of the corn snake are recognized. *Elaphe guttata guttata* is the "standard" corn snake and the subspecies to which the large majority of captive corn snakes belong. *Elaphe guttata emoryi,* the 'Great Plains rat snake', is the subspecies in the western areas of the species' range. Representatives of this subspecies have little or none of the red-orange color that is so common in *E. g. guttata* and are grey or brown animals with darker brown blotches. Some *E. g. emoryi* may also largely lack the black checks on the ventral scales. Its maximum recorded length is 60 inches (153 cm). Also, some specimens may have more blotches than are present in *E. g. guttata.* Some authors also consider the corn snakes from the Florida Keys as a separate subspecies, *Elaphe guttata rosacea* or the 'rosy rat snake'. These animals are characterized by a diminished amount of black pigment, both on the dorsal and ventral sides. The different subspecies of corn snake can be bred with one another successfully.

Geographic Range and Natural Habitat

The eastern subspecies of corn snake, *Elaphe guttata guttata,* naturally occurs throughout the southeastern United States from Louisiana through the Carolinas and Virginia and north as far as Maryland and southern New Jersey. The western subspecies, *Elaphe guttata emoryi,* occurs in Texas, northern Mexico, eastern New Mexico, and as far north as Kansas and Missouri. A disjunct population also occurs is part of eastern Utah and western Colorado.

Conant and Collins (1991, Peterson Field Guide Series, Houghton Mifflin Co., Boston) describes corn snakes as coming from a variety of terrestrial habitats including pine barrens, wood lots, rocky hillsides, etc. and are often more common than is apparent because they are secretive in nature and spend much of their time underground. Although they are capable climbers, they are generally encountered on the ground. Corn snakes are often diurnal (active during the day) in the spring but generally nocturnal (active at night) in warm weather.

Diet
In the wild, adult corn snakes feed on small rodents and birds in the wild which they suffocate by constriction. In captivity, they can subsist entirely on a diet of domestic mice (*Mus musculus*). Baby corn snakes in the wild may feed largely on small lizards and treefrogs, but in captivity, hatchlings are typically fed newborn mice.

Breeding Age and Longevity
Captive raised corn snakes are generally capable of reproducing in the second year after they hatch, though some may take until their third year and others may reproduce at less than one year of age. The minimum size of a sexually mature corn snake is probably in the area of two and a half feet (~75 cm) in length and about 100 g in weight and many corn snakes will well exceed this by the age of one and a half years. Corn snakes are capable of reproducing at least until the age of 10 years. The maximum recorded lifespan for a corn snake is 21 years.

Sexing adult corn snakes. The undersides of the tails of adult male and female amelanistic corn snakes clearly show the male's tail (left) remaining thick well past the vent while the female's tail tapers quickly. The anal scale (marking the vent) is the prominent half-moon scale that separates the single ventral scale on the underside of the body from the divided ventral scales on the underside of the tail.

5

Everting the hemipenes on a young male corn snake by the appropriate use
of pressure at the base of the tail.

 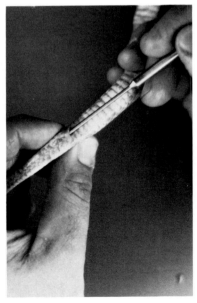

Probing male and female corn snakes. Note the difference in probe depth
between a female (right) and a male (left). Photo by Chris Estep.

Sexing

Adult corn snakes are easily sexed by examining the underside of the tails. The tails of females begin to taper immediately, or almost immediately, after the vent. The tails of males remain virtually untapered until well behind the vent. Males also have somewhat longer tails relative to their size.

Breeding and combat behavior are also reliable indicators of sex. See the section on breeding for details about these behaviors.

Hatchlings are also fairly easy to sex, though not readily by the above method. They are most simply sexed by applying a modest amount of pressure on the underside of the base of tail with one's thumb. This pressure is applied both downward and forward and is best done by "rolling" one's thumb forward over the base of the tail. This will evert the twin hemipenes of baby males. Females are distinguished by a failure to evert hemipenes. Errors in this method are typically falsely judging males to be females. The technique takes a little practice, and a few attempts may be needed, but is not very difficult once one has the hang of it. It is best taught or performed by an a person with experience with the technique.

Juveniles are potentially problematic to sex. As babies grow larger, they become more difficult and, eventually, impossible to sex by using pressure to evert the hemipenes. By this point in time the tail shape should be usable to distinguish the sexes though this may be more difficult than it is with adults.

Probes can be used to determine the sex of corn snakes of all ages. A blunt steel sexing probe of a size appropriate for the animal being sexed is inserted carefully through the vent and into the base of the tail. If the probe enters one of the two inverted hemipenes of the male, it can be inserted significantly farther than would be possible if the animal were a female. The use of a probe can injure a snake if performed incorrectly, and probing should be learned from someone with experience. Also, if a probe is too wide, it won't enter the hemipenal pocket of males resulting in males being erroneously sexed as females.

Choosing a Corn Snake

Selecting a corn snake to keep will mostly depend upon your own tastes as well as the selection of animals that may be available to you. Some guidelines that may be helpful in the selection process are given here.

Babies versus Adults

Buying hatchling and juvenile corn snakes has certain advantages over buying adults. They will typically be less expensive than an equivalent adult, they will generally be of known age and will potentially live longer than adults, something will often be known about their genetic pedigree, and there may be a greater variety to choose from. If you are interested in obtaining albinos or other selectively bred varieties of corn snakes you may find it difficult to obtain anything other than hatchlings. Young animals will also be less likely to have scars and less likely to be diseased or parasitized than wild-caught adults. Additionally, one can also get a certain satisfaction from raising a hatchling to adulthood.

But raising corn snakes from hatchlings also has definite disadvantages. Like infants of probably most species, hatchling corn snakes have a higher mortality rate than do young adults. They are more apt to be problem feeders, at least initially after hatching. It can also be more difficult to get appropriate food for them as they require newborn mice or small lizards. Hatchling corn snakes can be more expensive to feed than adults (at least if you do not raise your own mice). This is because they consume more feeder animals than do adults; combine this with the fact that pinky mice typically cost as much, or nearly as much, as adult mice. Expect to use about 100 feeder mice per corn snake for the first year and a half of its life. Another potential disadvantage of very young corn snakes is that their coloration is not the same as what it will be when they mature. You therefore will not be able to determine exactly what a baby will look like when it is an adult. Hatchlings pose another disadvantage to those interested in breeding corn snakes. Starting your collection with hatchlings can obviously delay the day when you produce your own hatchlings.

An excellent compromise between hatchlings and adults, when they can be found, are yearling corn snakes. Yearlings tend to have the same advantages as hatchlings but lack many of the disadvantages.

A six-month old female corn snake. This is an ideal size for an initial purchase.

Mutations Affecting Appearance

In addition to the considerable natural variation in appearance present between and within the subspecies of corn snakes, there are also several specific mutations affecting pigmentation and pattern that are selectively bred in captivity and that are popular alternatives to "normal" corn snakes. These heritable traits include the following:

Amelanism- Amelanistic animals are almost totally lacking the black/brown pigment melanin. Only a trace remains on the edge of the irises of the eyes, which are otherwise red. These are more commonly referred to as "albino" or "red albino" corn snakes. This simple recessive genetic trait is the most popular and widely available corn snake mutation.

Anerythrism- These animals are the complement of the amelanistics in that they have greys, browns, and black but lack red and orange. They are often referred to as "black" or "black albino" corn snakes. Anerythristic corn snakes

9

occur in the wild as a prominent minority of certain Florida populations. The aneryrithristic trait is caused by a recessive mutation.

Hypomelanism- Hypomelanistics are animals with a greatly reduced amount of melanin, but which are not lacking it completely. The pupils are black like normal animals. They vary from looking like particularly bright, attractive normal corns to looking close to being a black-eyed amelanistic. This trait is caused by a single recessive mutation.

Motley- The term coined to describe a mutation that produces irregular blotches that are often connected with one another. Additionally, the checkered ventral (belly) pattern is absent. The motley trait is caused by a recessive mutation.

Striped- Corn snakes that have their dorsal blotches replaced by four darkish stripes that run the length of the body. As in motley corn snakes, the ventral pattern is missing. This is another recessively inherited trait.

Zig-zag- An inherited trait that causes a variable tendency for the dorsal blotches to be connected to each other in a zig zag fashion. Probably caused by a recessive mutation.

Normal, snow and striped juvenile corn snakes in a plastic shoe box.

Other Corn Snake Varieties

In addition to the simple genetic traits described above, there are a few other "morphs" of corn snakes that are widely referred to. These include:

Blood Red- Blood Red corns (also sometimes simply called blood corns) as adults are a nearly patternless dark orange. The ventral checkered pattern is missing, replaced by irregular orange markings. The lack of ventral checks is a simple recessive trait, but the coloration is more complex in its inheritance.

Okeetee- This is a rather abused name that is often used to refer to corn snakes that have a considerable amount of orange in their ground color. The name originates from a hunting plantation in South Carolina reputed to have particularly attractive corn snakes.

Miami phase- Refers to the handsome corn snakes with red-orange blotches on a grey background that are especially prevalent around Miami, Florida.

Snow- The name given to the whitish corn snakes that combine the amelanistic and anerythristic mutations.

Ghost- The name given to the tannish or pinkish corn snakes that result from the combination of the mutations for hypomelanism and anerythrism.

Adult amelanistic (lighter) and anerythristic corn snakes.

11

Creamsicle- The amelanistic trait crossed into the *E. g. emoryi* subspecies. Paler orange than other amelanistic corn snakes.

Note: All captive-bred corn snake morphs will be presented in the companion book *"A Color Guide to Corn Snakes Captive-bred in the United States"* to be published by Advanced Vivarium Systems in August 1991.

The various mutations and morphs of corn snakes may vary considerably in availability and price. A good source of some of them are pet businesses that specialize in reptiles. Alternatively, a local herpetological society may be able to direct you to a local breeder or provide the addresses of out-of-state breeders that will ship animals. Utilizing the latter alternative, assumes that you are willing to incur overnight air freight expenses in addition to the purchase price of an animal and are willing to purchase an animal without having first seen it.

A couple of other points are worth mentioning here. First, keep in mind that the purchase price, especially for a normal corn snake, will be only a small part of the total cost of keeping the animal. A more expensive variety of corn snake will not be any more expensive to feed or house. And if you intend to breed corn snakes (or other snakes for that matter) keep in mind that valuable parents are generally required to produce valuable offspring that can be offered for sale. Also, keep in mind that the longer a strain has been around, the lower the price it can generally command.

Inbreeding

A caveat about non-natural varieties of corn snakes, especially the rarer and most expensive types, is that they may be quite inbred. Inbreeding (the breeding together of relatives) can be an essential part of producing and maintaining animals with specific traits. This is because most mutations are genetically recessive combined with the fact that a mutation may have originated historically from a single snake with the abnormal trait. Inbreeding exposes recessive mutations, both desirable ones, such as those that create an interesting color or pattern change, and the more numerous undesirable ones which can produce a variety of deleterious effects. These effects can include deformities, male sterility, diminished vigor, and shorter life expectancy. How much inbreeding can occur without problems can be quite variable. One generation of inbreeding is enough to produce some offspring with problems but sometimes many generations of inbreeding can be reasonably tolerated. The most common mutant strains of corn snakes, the amelanistic and anerythristic varieties, in general do not seem to suffer from obvious inbreeding defects. Other strains carrying mutations or otherwise selectively bred (e. g., blood red corns) ought to be regarded more cautiously. Given a choice between animals equivalent in other respects, it makes sense to select a corn snake that is the least inbred. If you wish to obtain a pair for breeding purposes, you may want to avoid getting siblings.

Inbreeding is not the only cause of health problems among hatchling corn snakes. Birth defects (hatch defects?) can be caused by improper conditions during egg incubation. Unlike problems from inbreeding, abnormalities caused by environmental insults to the embryo would not normally be expected to be heritable. There may also potentially be genetic incompatibilities between certain particular combinations of parents which could produce abnormal hatchlings. The risk to a human fetus with a Rh negative mother and a Rh positive father serves as an example of this possibility. I have heard of incidents with corn snakes consistent with parental incompatibility but I am not aware of incompatibility having been convincingly demonstrated.

Selecting a Potentially Healthy Corn Snake

Although it can never be guaranteed that any particular animal will be healthy and live a long life, there are steps that can be taken to minimize the chances of selecting a sickly corn snake. These steps include:

- **Feel for good muscle tone.** A corn snake should have a feeling of strength to it when it is being held. Avoid any animal that seems physically weak as weakness is an excellent indicator of ill health.

- **Select an animal with good body weight.** Avoid skinny animals that have a prominently visible backbone.

- **Look for attentiveness.** A corn snake should seem interested in its whereabouts when it is placed in your hands. This will manifest itself especially by tongue flicking behavior, and in most cases, by a distinct interest in moving about. Healthy animals may be reluctant to move about if their eyes are clouded blue in preparation for skin shedding.

- **Look for deformities and scars.** Check for kinks, bumps, and depressions along the backbone, especially near the tail. Scars may not be a health problem, but you may find that they detract from the animal.

- **Check for the presence of mites.** Mites are relatives of spiders. Many species of mites live by sucking blood. They can be seen as tiny dark round "bugs" crawling on the snake and possibly on your hand after handling an infested snake. They attach themselves to skin between the scales and around the edge of the eye. The mites that live on snakes will not feed on humans or other mammals. Captive-hatched baby corn snakes will seldom be seen with mites, but it is always wise to be on the alert for them. Avoid a mite infested animal unless you are prepared to quarantine it and treat it.

- **Check for signs of mouth or respiratory infections.** Signs of bubbly mucus from the mouth or nostrils will be a sign of respiratory illness. The inside of the mouth should be free of any sores or cheese-like matter which could be due to mouthrot.
- **Check the underside.** The vent should be externally clean and free of any encrustation. The belly should be free of any abnormal looking scales that might be a sign of a skin infection.

- **Check for any other obvious signs of problems.** Look for lumps on or in the body. Check that the eyes are clear and of equal size and color.

Additional Tips for Choosing a Hatchling

It is preferable to select a hatchling corn snake that has started feeding regularly on pinky (newborn) mice. Otherwise, you must be prepared to force feed or use lizards or lizard scented pinkies as food. If possible, ask to see the parents. This may help you predict what the coloration and temperament of the baby may be when it matures. It would also be worthwhile to verify that the parents are strong and vigorous animals. Don't be too concerned if a hatchling seems a little more nervous or aggressive than you would like. Calmer babies will probably make calmer adults, but baby corn snakes are to be expected to be distinctly more nervous than most captive adults. You might also want to consider getting more than one hatchling. Hatchling corn snakes, at least of the normal variety, are quite inexpensive, and having two would provide more assurance that at least one would survive. If both survived, you would have the option of keeping both and maybe breeding them, or you could keep only the one you thought had developed the best color and temperament.

Additional Tips for Choosing an Adult

There are fewer special concerns in choosing an adult, at least a captive-raised adult. If the animal is captive-raised, find out its age. It may be an old animal past its reproductive years as these are often gotten rid of by breeders. That may not necessarily matter to you if the animal is nicely priced, and you aren't interested in breeding it. Be aware that an adult (unless it was recently removed from the wild) should not be expected to improve appreciably in temperament. If it is too high strung for your tastes, it is best to avoid it. Also, be aware that the coloration of adults can change somewhat with time, though not nearly as much as a the changes that are often seen with babies. Generally, corn snakes seem to show their brightest coloration around the age of one or two years. After that age, the coloration of some adults may darken, and their pattern will tend to lose some contrast.

Housing and Maintenance

Prevent Escapes!

The first requirement for any snake in captivity is an escape-proof cage. This is hard to emphasize enough. Quite possibly, more beginners lose their snakes through their escaping than through their deaths. Snakes are ideally shaped for having long reaches and are capable of crawling through very small openings. Compared to many snakes, corn snakes are fairly slender and are good climbers, both being traits that may make them better than average escape artists. Fortunately, terrariums suitable for snakes can now be found in many pet stores. These can be glass tanks with either a hinged top or a sliding screen top or they may be Plexiglas enclosures with sliding doors in front. If you choose to put a lid on a fish tank, you should probably build a heavy and secure lid yourself rather than buy a commercial lid that was probably intended as a cover for cages housing small mammals. When constructing your own lid, try to design it such that an extra weight, or being locked, is not essential to its functioning. Locks are great but most of us sometimes forget to use them. Be especially careful with cages intended to house hatchling corn snakes. Even some of the cages designed and sold to house snakes may have small gaps at corners large enough for a baby corn snake to slip through. Wiggle the lid around to see if any such gaps can be found and take corrective measures as necessary.

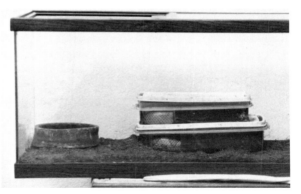

A simple vivarium setup for adult corn snakes. This 15 gallon tank has the necessary minimum cage requirements: locking lid, water bowl, substrate (potting soil in this case), shelters, and a source of heat (supplied here by a heating pad under part of the enclosure).

Enclosure Setup for Adults

Even the largest corn snake can be housed adequately in a 15 gallon (57 liter) terrarium (typical measurements: 1' by 1' by 2'). Larger cages of course allow more room to move about and are recommended when keeping more than one corn snake. A number of different substrates can be suitable for use in a corn snake cage. Potting soil, pine chips (not cedar, which can be toxic), newspaper or the "astroturf" that comes with many commercial terrariums can all be suitable and readily cleaned of feces. If you use "astroturf", be sure that, after being washed, it is fully dry before being placed back in a cage. A water bowl should be present in the cage at all times. Unlike some snakes, corn snakes do not seem inclined to soak in their water bowls, so a small container is all that is required.

Having one or more shelters to serve as hiding places within the cage is highly recommended. Although this has the advantage of reducing stress to the animal, it may mean that the animal is seldom seen. Corn snakes will spend the majority of their time staying in shelters in captivity, as they presumably would also do in the wild. If seeing an animal without removing it from the cage is an important priority, one could use translucent plastic hideboxes. Additionally, one might want to initially choose an individual corn snake that does not seem at all skittish when being handled, as these are less likely to be shy and retiring.

The substrate alone may allow the animal to conceal itself. A snake may root its way underneath its wood chips or its astroturf for example. Corn snakes are not normally very inclined to burrow into soil if they have been provided with a shelter. Shelters can be constructed from any appropriately sized box or container such as paper milk cartons or plastic food storage containers with holes cut in them or hollow logs. A good size for shelters is fairly small, with room for only a small number of animals. One can also purchase attractive commercially produced shelters made to look like natural rocks. The important features of any shelter are that it is reasonably dry, either easily cleaned or easily replaced, and that it does not present any hazard of falling onto and injuring the animal (as might, for example, a pile of rocks). Another useful idea is to have a shelter in a warm spot of the enclosure and an additional shelter in a cooler area so that the animal has a choice of temperatures to select from when hiding.

Corn snakes may be housed separately or in small groups. Housing a number of corn snakes together is not normally a problem. However, one should be alert for combat between males during the breeding season, and one should always separate animals for feeding purposes. New animals should be kept separate from established animals to ensure that the newcomers are healthy and not likely to transmit mites or other diseases. Prevention of mite infestations is much preferable to trying to eradicate them.

Temperature or Heating

Corn snakes, especially young ones, should have daily access to temperatures between 75°-85° F (25°-30° C)) in order to do well. For this reason, they should be provided with a heat source, at least for a large part of days when they are not intentionally being hibernated. There are a number of ways that this extra heat can be provided. The natural heat from a warm summer climate may be sufficient at many times of the year. Usually though, a supplemental heat source will be needed. The goal in heating a cage is to provide a choice of temperatures for the animal. A standard heating pad, set on low, is an excellent means of accomplishing this. It can be placed underneath one half

A setup for keeping a number of hatchling and juvenile corn snakes. Shelves are heated with heat tape (adjusted with dimmer switch) sitting underneath aluminum sheet metal. Shelves are spaced to prevent lids of individual plastic shoe boxes from being pushed up by snakes. Individual boxes can be outfitted simply with paper towel, a water bowl, and a shelter.

(not under all!) of small and medium sized terrariums and will provide warmth through a moderate thickness of substrate. Be careful not to damage the heating pad with too much weight on part of the pad. Commercially produced heating pads designed specifically for use with reptile cages are also now available in several sizes and are ideal for heating many types of reptile enclosures. Commercial "hot rock" type heaters can be used, but may not be waterproof and may be capable of burning animals that sit on them for long periods. It may be desirable to bury the hot rocks in the substrate in a way that will disperse the heat. If other heat sources are not available, an incandescent lamp can provide some heat. However, it will consume more electricity and will probably warm corn snakes less efficiently than would a heating pad. Corn snakes are also less inclined to bask under a light than are some other snakes.

Although the major concerns when housing a snake involve the enclosure itself, there are also a couple of points worth considering about the room in which the enclosure is kept. For example, you may wish to set up your cages in a room that you don't mind keeping cool during the winter. As is described in a later section, winter cooling is useful for breeding corn snakes. Additionally, it is wise to plan for the possibility that a corn snake may escape from its cage. If possible, place a snake enclosure in a room that offers the best chance of finding a missing snake.

Enclosure Setup for Hatchlings and Juveniles.

Cages for young corn snakes should include the same basic elements as cages for adults, namely substrate, water, shelter, warmth, and being escape-proof. Providing adequate heat is particularly important for baby corn snakes in order to aid the rapid digestion of their meals. Even a newborn mouse can weigh 25% of the body weight of a hatchling corn snake and is a potentially difficult-to-digest meal. Hatchlings not kept adequately warm will be much more prone to regurgitate meals. Rapid growth of hatchlings and juveniles will also depend upon keeping the animals sufficiently warm. The preferred temperature range of baby corn snakes appears to be between 80° and 90° F (27°-32° C), and temperatures within this range should always be available to them in at least part of their cage. Keep in mind however, that while cool temperatures are not desirable, temperatures that are too high can quickly kill.

It is preferable to house hatchling corn snakes individually in order to reduce stress and monitor their progress. This will also reduce the chances of infectious diseases ever becoming a problem. It can also be very important at feeding time. Baby corn snakes, especially initially, can be nervous and uncertain about eating. They often need to be left alone with their intended meal for a fair length of time before they will eat. This can be dangerous if more than one baby is present and two begin eating the same meal starting from opposite ends. Unless caught in time, this can lead to one baby swallowing and killing the other. The swallower can also be killed by this. If you intend to breed corn snakes, you must be prepared to house and feed a considerable number of hatchlings. A common means among breeders to house hatchling corn snakes is to keep them individually in very small plastic containers such as those that cottage cheese is sold in. All that is needed are a few small holes for ventilation and some moss that is occasionally misted with water to keep it humid. In very humid climates, it may not even be necessary to mist. Very small containers like this can have the advantage that a hatchling will find it difficult to ignore an intended meal, something much more likely in a more spacious cage. Another common cage setup for hatchling and juvenile snakes makes use of plastic shoe boxes. A paper towel and a small water bowl on the inside, and a reliable way of keeping the lid on, are the minimal requirements for these "cages". Plastic shoe boxes are small enough to be able to conveniently keep a sizable number of them, yet large enough to house a young corn snake for a year or more of growth. Such shoe box cages are best kept on shelves built with two special features. First, the distance between of the shelves should be just high enough to accommodate the height of the shoe boxes. If built correctly, such shelves will provide a fail safe means of preventing the snakes from pushing up their lids and escaping. Second, the setup should have a strip of heat tape running along each shelf to provide heat. The heat tape must be connected to a rheostat for adjusting temperature and can be put either on the underside of the shelf or on the top side underneath a thin sheet of aluminum. The sheet metal serves to disperse the heat over a wider area which is good for the snakes and necessary to ensure the heat tape does not become a fire hazard. The front side of the boxes provides the cool end either by hanging out from the shelves or by not lying on top of the heated sheet metal. If most snakes are seen at the cool end, the rheostat can be adjusted lower. A cool end in a cage provides important insurance against the possibility that an animal will become lethally over-heated. Keep a thermometer in a cage to monitor the temperature and make adjustments with the rheostat with care. Electronic thermostats with a sensor placed inside one of the shoe boxes are ideal for monitoring temperatures with this type of setup.

Handling Corn Snakes

Corn snakes are among the most easily handled and most recommended of all pet snakes. Adult corn snakes in captivity are typically calm and rather slow moving animals that are readily handled without any of the biting, thrashing around, defecating, or musking that is sometimes seen in other snakes. Some adults are rather high strung and jumpy, but many more are calm to the point of seeming completely unperturbable.

Some baby corn snakes are also quite calm right from hatching. Many others though, tend to be quite nervous and will often vibrate their tails and may sometimes bite. When handled, baby corn snakes may try to dive out of one's hands, and care should be taken to prevent this. Don't restrain a nervous baby snake by suddenly grasping it so tightly that it can't move. This may elicit a bite. Instead, grasp it firmly enough to slow, but not stop, its movement. An alarmed hatchling may also defecate if restrained too much, a behavior that is rare if the animal is handled gently, and one that should disappear altogether as the animal grows older.

Any tendency for corn snakes of any age to bite is likely to be due largely to the animal being afraid. The first sign of alarm shown by a corn snake will generally be vibration of its tail. Many species of snakes, despite lacking a rattle, will rapidly vibrate the tips of their tails when alarmed in a manner reminiscent of rattlesnakes. Against many surfaces, this tail vibration may be plainly audible. A further state of alarm will typically be accompanied by the snake coiling, flattening its head, and poising to strike. Anything moving too close and too quickly toward the animal in such an excited state is likely to be struck at. Corn snake bites are quick strikes and releases accompanied by a momentary little hiss. Their jaws cannot exert any appreciable biting pressure, but their teeth, though small, are very sharp and can produce numerous pinprick-like wounds. It can be rather amusing to see a tiny corn snake go through this defensive posturing to threaten one of your hands, when at the same time it is being held in your other hand.

If you have a corn snake that is easily alarmed, try to act in a way that will ease its fears. Be sure to have a shelter in the animal's cage. Avoid sudden movements near the snake. When preparing to handle the animal, present your hand to it slowly and allow it to flick its tongue on you. Your scent will allow it to recognize you and the snake should come to regard its presence as non-threatening. Some individuals are innately more fearful and shy than others and will never become completely relaxed.

Use extra care when handling snakes that have recently eaten. Individuals that become especially stressed by handling might regurgitate their meal.

Corn Snakes and Black Holes

Corn snakes seem to enjoy getting out of their cages and exploring their surroundings. They will crawl about and investigate new things at their leisure with no obvious intent of escaping. If you allow your corn snake out of its cage do not be lulled into a false sense of security by their nonchalance. There is probably nothing they would rather do than find a dark hole and crawl into it.

Be prepared to extract your animal from underneath your most immovable furniture or from out of whatever dark hole the snake may have discovered. Don't set a small corn snake in your bathroom sink while you clean its cage. It may immediately crawl down the drain. In short, anticipate mischief if a snake is ever out of its cage. If you ever catch a corn snake that is halfway into some hole-of-no-return, grab its remaining body tightly enough to prevent any further movement into the hole, but don't try to yank it out quickly. Hold on tightly and be patient. You will slowly, but surely, win the tug-of-war as the snake tires and decides enough is enough.

Corn snakes seem to consider being out of their cage not only a good time to explore but also a good time to defecate. This is mostly a concern when the animal is out and has some undisturbed time to itself rather than when the snake is being handled. If you allow your corn snake out you may wish to choose times soon after the animal has defecated in its cage or times when the snake has not eaten recently.

Great Plains rat snake *(Elaphe guttata emoryi)* constricting a thawed mouse.

Feeding and Growth of Corn Snakes

Feeding Adults

Adult corn snakes are most easily maintained by feeding them entirely on a diet of commercially-raised mice. No nutritional supplements are needed provided the mice themselves have been fed a nutritious diet. Mice raised as food for snakes will usually have been fed commercial mouse chow and should be adequately nutritious. Some people that breed mice may use less nutritious food for their rodents and, I'm told, snakes fed on such ill-fed mice may be obese looking and not breed well. Wild-caught rodents, such as those occasionally caught by the family cat, would certainly be eaten by corn snakes, but potentially could carry parasites that might be passed to snakes. It is probably best to avoid ever giving them to your snakes.

Baby and small juvenile mice may be swallowed live by corn snakes, but larger mice will be killed by constriction before being eaten. Constriction involves the corn snake seizing the mouse in its jaws and very rapidly coiling around the mouse to immobilize and suffocate it. After the mouse has ceased struggling, the snake will gradually loosen its grip and begin searching via tongue flicking for the head of the mouse, which will almost always be what is swallowed first.

Many people recommend against feeding live adult mice to snakes because the mice are capable of biting and injuring the snake. However, the probability of an adult corn snake being seriously injured by a mouse it is constricting is probably very low however. Pre-killing or pre-stunning mice is certainly not a bad idea, and if larger or more powerfully jawed rodents are ever used, it is wiser still to pre-kill them. It is also best not to leave medium or large mice unattended in a snake's cage. If the snake does not kill the mouse, the mouse may eventually chew upon the snake and harm it. At the very least, put a pellet of mouse chow in the cage also.

One of the conveniences of keeping corn snakes over some other reptiles is that they will generally feed on pre-killed animals, including ones that have been previously frozen (but thoroughly thawed!). The potential advantages of frozen mice include: keeping a sizable supply of mice around without the inconvenience of having to care for live mice; a lower cost per mouse if mice are bought in large numbers; not having to watch mice be killed each time you feed your snakes.

Frozen mice can be thawed by leaving them at room temperature for an hour or more, preferably on a surface that conducts heat well. A heating pad, or setting the mice on a good heat conducting surface, can accelerate the thawing process. Soaking in warm water also works well but, of course, leaves the mice wet. Microwaving frozen mice is not recommended as this will cook the extremities before thawing is complete and these "nuked" mice will probably be rejected by corn snakes. Most adult corn snakes will eat thawed mice with gusto, seizing and constricting them as they would live mice especially if the mouse is held by the tail and wiggled around in front of the snake. Some individuals are fussier however and are best fed by leaving the snake alone for a while with one or more thawed mice. Offering several thawed mice simultaneously (easy to do if you are feeding a number of snakes) or both fuzzy and weaned mice (some corn snakes prefer one or the other) can sometimes be helpful in getting these connoisseurs to eat their TV dinners.

Always separate adults to feed them. If two corn snakes seize the same mouse, whether live or frozen, they will instantly be wrapped around both the mouse and one another. A corn snake will not normally release its jaws from an intended meal that it is constricting until after the prey has ceased moving. If two snakes have the same mouse, each will feel the other struggling, and both will tenaciously refuse to release their grips. Prevent this from happening at all costs. Be careful too, if, for example, you feed thawed mice to two snakes on opposite sides of a sizable cage. Even though both may initially be engrossed in their own constriction, after one animal ceases its constriction, it may be more attracted to the motion of the feeding animal on the other side of its cage than it is to the dead mouse sitting right under its nose.

Feeding Hatchling Corn Snakes

The most appropriate food for hatchling corn snakes are pinky (newborn) mice. Once acclimated, hatchling corn snakes can consume pinky mice every two to five days with the size of the feeder animals increasing as the snakes grow. Less frequent feeding is sufficient to keep the animals healthy, but growth will obviously be slower.

Some general guidelines when trying to begin feeding baby corn snakes should include:
1. Be sure to keep the snake warm.

2. Place the hatchling in a small enough container so that it will readily encounter the intended meal.

3. When possible, keep hatchlings separated to avoid having two animals grab the same food item and to avoid having more timid individuals get intimidated.

4. Provide a shelter or other place for the snake to conceal itself.

5. Keep food items small. Small items are more easily digested than larger items. A general guideline would be to offer a single mouse of about the same girth as the snake. Regurgitation of food is often more frequent with hatchlings than with adults and is much more likely with large meals than with small meals. Once a hatchling is well established at eating, one can increase meal size.

6. Some hatchling corn snakes may feed as soon as they emerge from the egg but most probably won't. Don't feel compelled to try to feed hatchlings until after they shed for the first time which will occur a week or two after hatching.

7. Corn snakes should start feeding within a month or so of hatching. Starvation probably wouldn't occur for several more weeks but it is best to have animals feeding as early as possible. How long hatchlings can survive without starving is probably quite variable depending upon how much yolk reserve the snake has at hatching, the temperature the animal is kept at, and how active the animal is.

Problem Feeders

A significant percentage of hatchling corn snakes will begin eating newborn mice without problems and once started, will generally continue to feed without problems. However, many hatchlings may be reluctant to start feeding on mice. A list of means to feed such difficult hatchlings is given below. The intent of all these techniques is to keep the snake alive until it acquires a taste for mice. The techniques are basically of two types, either using a food item with an altered scent or force feeding.

Bob Applegate, a breeder of a variety of snakes, has listed the following steps he has used to get babies started:

1. Place live pinky mouse in with the hatchling snake for a few hours, if uneaten, replace for a while with a dead pinky.

2. Wash a pinky in soap and water, rinse and dry, then present to the hatchling. Try live, then a dead one. Washing apparently can remove some scent that can inhibit eating by some hatchling snakes.

3. Rub a pinky with a small lizard such as *Anolis*, *Uta* or *Sceloporus* (anoles, side-blotched and fence lizards, respectively) to transfer some of the scent. Place a moistened section of a skin or shed skin from a lizard on the head and back of a pre-killed pinky. A lizard kept frozen can be a good source of bits of skin.

4. Offer a small live lizard. Small lizards, such as anoles, are probably the major food of most hatchling corn snakes in the wild and many captive hatchlings will eat small lizards even when they show no interest in pinky mice. Feeding snakes with lizards may present some problems. They can be relatively expensive to purchase and may carry diseases or parasites which could be transmitted to a snake. If hatchlings start on lizards, every effort should be made to get them to switch to mice as soon as possible.

If different techniques to get a hatchling feeding voluntarily fail, force-feeding can be resorted to. For this purpose, some herpetoculturists use a large heavy-duty metal syringe (referred to as a pinky pump) to force-feed baby snakes. Dead pinkies are placed into the syringe and forced out as a slurry through the end that is placed down the snake's throat. This technique has the disadvantages of requiring an expensive syringe and not delivering food in very continuous fashion. Sudden spurts of food in the throat of a little snake can be injurious. An alternative is to use a standard syringe with a few inches of stiff, narrow tubing at the end to force feed finely ground and strained cat food or meat baby food. These emergency-use foods are cheap, come in small containers, are very fine in consistency, and are infrequently regurgitated. However, baby food, and perhaps cat food as well, are probably not nutritionally sufficient to feed snakes indefinitely. When force feeding using a syringe, hold the sides of the snake's head with the thumb and forefinger of the left hand while the other fingers of that hand keep the neck and upper body straight. The tube (with end cut at an angle) can then be used to pry open the snake's mouth, and the tube is slid down the throat at least an inch. About 1 cc per meal will mimic the volume of a small pinky. There is little danger of putting the tube down the snake's airway because the opening for this is very small and near the front of the lower jaw.

Another force-feeding technique that is widely used is to force-feed hatchlings 1/2" to 3/4" sections of tail from pre-killed mice. These can be pushed directly down into the throats of hatchling snakes. Often, hatchlings will start swallowing tail sections placed in the throat area. Baby corn snakes can also be force-fed whole dead newborn pinky mice. Use as small of a pinky as possible and lubricate it first with a little water. After gently prying open the snake's mouth, put the head of the pinky as far back in the mouth as possible. Occasionally, the snake may begin to voluntarily swallow it. If not, the pinky can be steadily, but very carefully, pushed down the snake's throat. Once fully into the mouth of the snake, a small blunt "ramrod" may be needed to push the pinky completely into the throat. Either the head of a nail or the pocket clip on the plastic cap of a ball point pen can be suitable for this purpose. The snake will not be too happy about being force-fed and care should be taken that it does not regurgitate the intended meal which is what the snake will be trying to do. One should be holding on to the snake's head at all times. Once well into the snake's throat, the pinky can be massaged down further toward the stomach. At this point the snake will probably have ceased trying to regurgitate the pinky and may well push it toward its stomach on its own.

A useful tactic with corn snakes of all ages that are reluctant to eat thawed mice is to tap the thawed mouse against the side of the body (but not against the head or neck). In hatchlings, this may elicit a defense strike that can be followed, if the snake is not startled, by the pinky being eaten. In older animals, this "tease feeding" may need to be somewhat more aggressive in order to work. Tapping the thawed mouse firmly against the side or neck, even to the extent that seems like harassment, may be effective at eliciting either a bite or partial constriction which may in turn be followed by the mouse being eaten. Finicky individuals vary widely in how they react to this; some respond well, and others may seem terrorized by it.

Another trick that can be useful with older corn snakes that are hesitant to feed on thawed mice involves putting a second thawed mouse into the still open mouth of an animal just finishing a first meal. The snake will generally keep swallowing until it has consumed both food items.

Growth of Juvenile Corn Snakes

Conant (1975, Peterson Field Guide Series, Houghton Mifflin Co., Boston) describes hatchling corn snakes as being 9-14 in. (23-36 cm) in total length. Typical corn snake hatchlings are in the low end of this range with only the offspring of E. guttata emoryi females generally approaching 14 in. (36 cm). In terms of weight, typical corn snake hatchlings are 5-10 g, and the range that I have seen is 3-19 g..

Eating is generally at a quite steady pace throughout the time the babies remain in well heated enclosures. Rapidly growing baby corn snakes can assimilate more than 40% of the weight of their food into their own body weight. Figure 1 shows a semi-logarithmic graph of the weight gain of a number of rapidly growing babies that the author has raised. This type of graph has the advantage of showing a constant rate of weight doubling as a straight line and allows one to better appreciate the rapid growth of young animals. It can be seen from this figure that growth is often at a near constant rate for much of the first year. For these five individuals, the shortest period of time required to double in weight (maintained for a minimum of three months) varies from 1.4 to 2.2 months. It is possible that at temperatures somewhat higher than 82 F - 86 F (28 C - 30 C) that growth rates might be higher still. In four of the animals, the growth rate can be seen to drop off noticeably after the juveniles reach

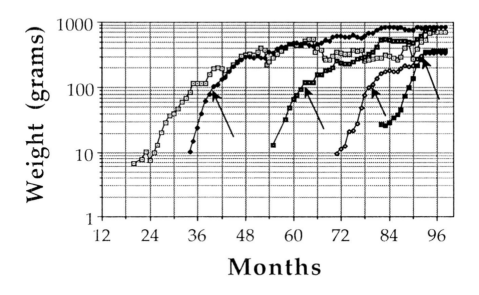

Figure 1. **Semi-logarithmic plot of the growth of five corn snakes from near-hatchling size to adulthood.** Numbered months represent the January of each year during the seven year interval shown. Arrows indicate the point in time when the juvenile snakes were shifted from "baby boxes" to the somewhat cooler cages where adults are kept..

about 100 g in weight. In one case, this is because the animal was shifted to a winter cooling period. In the other three cases, it is apparently due to shifting the animals from their "baby boxes" to the cooler cages where they were to be housed with adults (the time of this shift is indicated by arrows). The one animal that was kept longer in its baby box maintained a high rate of growth well past 100 g. The temperature shifts demonstrate convincingly the importance of warm temperatures to rapid growth in young corn snakes.

Winter Cooling of Adult Corn Snakes

Like other snakes from temperate climates, corn snakes in the wild are affected by seasonal changes in the weather. They are inactive in cool or cold winter weather and the warmer spring weather serves as a cue for the animals to initiate breeding behavior and resume feeding. People intending to breed their corn snakes will typically attempt to partially mimic tne seasons by exposing their snakes to a period of cooler temperatures, and then following that with a spring warm-up, in order to stimulate and synchronize the breeding behavior of their animals. The spring rise in temperature probably serves as the stimulus that spurs reproduction.

The use of a winter cooling period with adult corn snakes leads to a pronounced annual cycle in the lives of the animals. A reasonable way to think of this cycle is to picture it composed of four parts. The first part, often lasting a few months, is the winter cooling, where no feeding or breeding occur, but which functions to induce and synchronize breeding. This winter cooling period, technically considered "brumation", is generally referred to as "hibernation" despite the fact that it is not a true hibernation. The second part, the post-hibernation period, is the period where the temperature is first raised and most animals resume feeding, but do not yet engage in breeding behavior. This typically lasts about a month and perhaps could be said to end when animals have their first post-hibernation skin shedding. The third part of the annual cycle is the breeding season during which mating and egg-laying occur, and both sexes typically go through a lengthy period of time with little or no eating. Once egg-laying is completed for the year, about six months after the end of hibernation, all individuals generally will be feeding at their maximum rates which often continues until the next winter's cool period. This fourth and last part of the year could be referred to as the feeding season although its boundary with the breeding season is at best vague.

Snakes that live naturally in areas with long and cold winters may require a long and cold winter cooling period in order to reproduce. Corn snakes largely live in areas with relatively mild winters and do not require drastic cooling in order to breed and lay eggs with regularity. And at least some reproduction can occur in the absence of any cooling period. However, given that a winter cooling period for corn snakes can constitute no more than turning off their supplemental heat and not feeding them for a period of time, it is well worth recommending to anyone wishing to reproduce corn snakes and probably worth considering even for people without interest in breeding their animal(s).

Some individual corn snakes may largely stop eating in the fall whether or not they are exposed to a cool period. A cool period can also serve a snake keeper as a welcome respite from the routine of frequently feeding a number of snakes.

The information in the following sections has largely been generated from my own group of corn snakes. For each of the last several years, my adult animals (1 1/2 years old and up) have been cooled off for approximately three months during the winter. By late November, I begin to shorten the daily time period during which the heating pads are on. Be early December, all heating is turned off until the end of the hibernation period. Temperatures during this time vary somewhat but generally are between 63°-72° F (17°-22° C). No food is given to the animals until the end of the cooling period despite the fact that many of the animals might still be interested in eating. One should avoid rapidly cooling animals that have recently eaten in order to provide them time to completely digest their last meal. Water should always be available during the winter cool period.

There is typically little activity during the cool period despite the fact that the temperatures that my corn snakes experience are not very low. The animals spend the great majority of their time in their boxes. If the temperature climbs above about 68° F (20° C) I will usually notice some animals beginning to crawl about. These low activity levels combined with the cool temperature allow the snakes to go through hibernation with a minimum of weight loss. From my own measurements, on average, adults of all sizes with normal fat reserves, unless they shed their skin, lose only 1.6% of their body weight from mid-December to mid-January and lose only an additional 0.7% of their body weight between mid-January to mid-February. A shed skin, if it occurs, will produce an additional 3% weight loss. The greater and more variable weight loss observed during the first part of the hibernation period is probably at least partly caused by variable amounts of food that may be eliminated from the guts of the animals soon after the start of hibernation. Frequently, an animal will display a slight weight gain for a given month during hibernation despite not having eaten. This presumably is due to the snake having recently drank some water. Particularly skinny corn snakes will lose weight much more rapidly than animals with normal fat reserves. In seven instances of overwintering skinny corn snakes (18% to 51% below previous peak weights) I have measured an average rate of weight loss of 7% over two months (compared to 2.3% for healthy animals). This faster weight loss is probably largely due to the skinny animals burning carbohydrate and protein reserves rather than burning fat reserves as fat provides approximately twice as many calories per unit weight as carbohydrates or protein. The *absolute* rate of weight loss of the skinny animals is about double that of corn snakes of the same length.

Toward the end of February, I begin to phase in the daily heating cycle again, and by the beginning of March, I resume feeding of the animals.

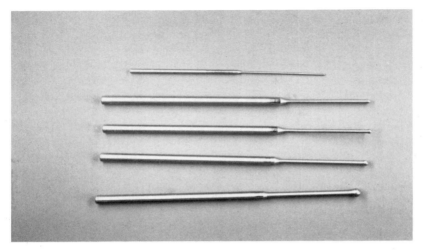

A set of sexing probes. The smaller probe is suitable for sexing subadult corn snakes. Photo by Chris Estep.

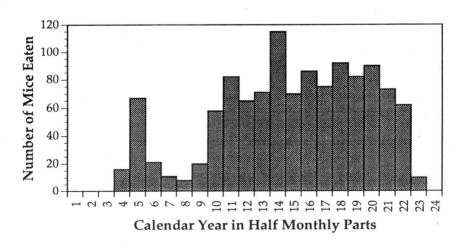

Figure 2. **Total eating of my hibernated adult male corn snakes over a five year period.** Numbers refer to 1/2 monthly periods beginning in January (for example, period 16 is the last half of August).

Feeding and Growth Patterns of Hibernated Adults

Males

Unlike the feeding of babies, the feeding of adult corn snakes that have been winter cooled is not spread evenly throughout the year. This is only partly due to food being withheld from them during hibernation. Figure 2 shows the annual distribution of the feeding of hibernated males with the year broken down into 24 half-monthly periods. On average, a modest amount of feeding occurs within the few weeks after coming out of the hibernation period. Some individuals may eat well, and others may not eat at all. Soon after this, generally following their first skin sloughing of the year, males cease eating for one to two months during the peak of the breeding season. Eating typically resumes after this period and is generally maintained at a more or less steady pace until the subsequent hibernation period. Over the course of a calendar year, males consume 25 to 50 mice which, for average sized males, is very roughly the equivalent to consuming their own weight in food per year.

All the adult males that I have kept and that have been hibernated have more or less displayed the characteristic feeding pattern shown in Figure 2. However, some variation has been observed and is worth noting. Young adult males for instance appear to feed somewhat more than older males both before and during the breeding season. Some males may not eat at all during this time. One particular male of mine, at least in the last couple of years, has not resumed eating until about a month after the other males have resumed eating.

The uneven distribution throughout the year of eating and activity leads to the weights of males displaying a clear yearly cycle. This yearly pattern includes minimal hibernation weight loss followed by a small gain during the spring warm-up period, an often sharp weight loss during the breeding season, and finally, weight recovery after the breeding season. Younger males, as already mentioned, tend to eat more before and even during the breeding season than do larger and older males and show minimal weight loss or modest weight gain during the breeding season. The larger, older males, in contrast, invariably lose weight during the breeding season.

During periods of the breeding season when they are not eating, I have measured males to lose weight at an average rate of 6.3% per month (4.0% per

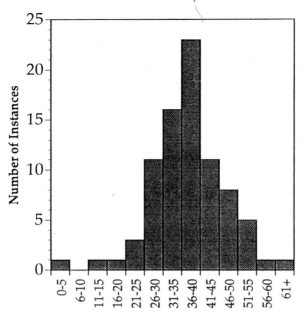

Number of Days Without Eating Prior to Laying Eggs

Figure 3. **The length of time that female corn snakes fast immediately prior to laying their eggs.**

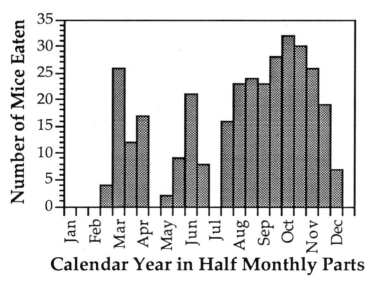

Calendar Year in Half Monthly Parts

Figure 4A **Feeding of hibernated adult female corn snakes.** Five years of eating of an *Elaphe guttata guttata* female.

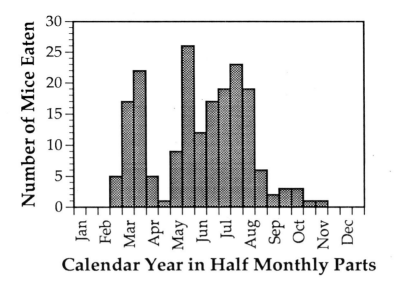

Figure 4B. Four years of eating of an *Elaphe guttata emoryi* female.

month when correcting for shed skins), a distinctly faster rate than occurs during the non-feeding period of hibernation. In addition to skin shedding, other factors that contribute to this relatively rapid weight loss include: transfer of semen during mating, being at a higher average temperature (which raises their metabolic rate), and being, on average, distinctly more active during this period. More will be said of this in the section on breeding.

Females

The annual feeding pattern of typical adult females could be summarized as being composed of more or less continuous eating broken only by periods of non-eating immediately prior to egg laying. As shown in Figure 3, this pre-egg-laying fasting period generally lasts from 25 to 50 days. Females that I have kept have been observed to eat between 30 and 75 adult mice per year. Producing eggs obviously requires that females take in more calories than males when all else is equal.

As with the males, some differences between the yearly feeding cycles of individual females are present. For example, as will be described in a later section, not all females have the same egg-laying schedule, and non-feeding periods are shifted accordingly. Perhaps the most radically different feeding pattern observed for a female that I have kept is shown in Figure 4. Figure 4A shows a typical yearly feeding pattern of a female corn snake, in this case an animal that always lays two clutches of eggs per year. Figure 4B shows the yearly feeding pattern of a Great Plains rat snake (*Elaphe guttata emoryi*) female. This representative of the western subspecies of the corn snake often lays two clutches of eggs per year, but essentially ceases eating by the end of August, three months earlier than the other females. This suggests that this animal is adapted to an environment with a shorter warm season. Unfortunately, I do not know from where in its range this individual originated and knowing that it comes from a pet shop in Tucson is of no help! Figure 5 shows a graph of the weight changes of these two individual females over the years that I have had them. The heavier spring eating relative to males, and the early cessation of eating of the *E. g. emoryi* female is apparent. Also visible in Figure 5 is the fact that, if a second clutch of eggs is laid during a given year, invariably the female snake is lighter in weight and consequently lays a smaller clutch the second time around.

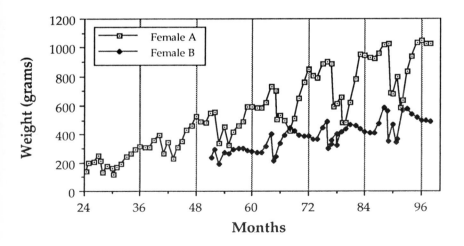

Figure 5. **Weight records of two female corn snakes (the same individuals of Figure 4).** Vertical lines indicate the January of each year.

Breeding and Egg-Laying

Breeding Season

The breeding season is rather sharply defined for female corn snakes. It begins with their first post-hibernation shed skin. Of the 50 or so copulations that I have observed over a several year period, apparently none involved females that had not yet had their first post-hibernation molt. Two exceptions where I have no record of a prior shed are almost certainly due to simply not noting the molt's occurrence in my records. Occasionally, though, I have seen a male show some interest in mating with a female that has yet to have her post-hibernation shed. Given that male snakes are attracted to the "scent" of a pheromone present on the skin of reproductive females, it is not surprising that the removal of an old skin layer through molting would lead to the females instantly becoming more attractive to males. Likewise, the end of the breeding season for a female corn snake appears to be fairly abrupt as well and occurs about 20 days prior to laying their eggs. This corresponds to a point in time about a week before the pre-egglaying shed. Matings appear to be uniformly spread out between these two borders (which are about one month, or sometimes up to two months apart). A second "breeding season" will occur for females if they are to lay a second clutch of eggs. This second season seems much less pronounced however, as only about 10% of the copulations that I have observed have occurred during this second season despite second clutches accounting for a third of the total egg clutches that I have observed. The borders of this second breeding season are likely to be equivalent to the borders of the first breeding season, the start occurring with the third shed skin of the year (10-14 days after laying of the first clutch), and the end occurring sometime before the next shed (the fourth of the year).

Unlike the situation with female corn snakes, the breeding season for males is not very sharply defined. Typically, mating occurs after the male has shed for the first time, however, I have noted bona fide exceptions. In one instance, a male copulated two days before his first shed of the season, and in another instance, a male copulated four days before his first shed (with eyes still clouded). Having shed is clearly not essential as far as the male corn snake is concerned. How long into the year males remain capable of mating is not completely clear to me. I have observed mating to occur as late as four months after the start of the post-hibernation warm-up.

As perhaps should be expected, some males are distinctly more interested in mating than are other males. Additionally, not all females are equally attractive to males. I have had some difficulties at times, for example, finding a male willing to mate with my *Elaphe guttata emoryi* female. The last couple of years I have resorted to trickery to ensure that she bred. When a male that I was interested in breeding to the *E. g. emoryi* female was busy ardently courting another female I would switch females on him, and he would then mate with the *E. g. emoryi* female. With the original female and the *E. g. emoryi* female both present, the male would always choose to court the original. It may be that the skin pheromone of the female may be slightly different between the eastern and western subspecies. I also have the impression that large females are more attractive to males. This would make some evolutionary sense since mating with a larger female would likely result in producing more offspring. Although I have no old female corn snakes yet, I would suppose that females past their reproductive years would not be courted by males. It has not been possible for me to tell if female corn snakes discriminate between potential mates. With a more passive role in mating, any such discrimination by females might typically be of a subtle nature. However, I have been told by another corn snake breeder, Rich Zuchowski, that he has seen a female vigorously flee from a male into whose cage she had been introduced. On the other hand, the same female, remained passive toward the advances of a second male when placed in another cage, suggesting that female corn snakes can sometimes be actively discriminating.

Courtship Behavior

The courtship behavior of corn snakes is similar to that of other colubrid snakes and has been described in a detailed fashion along with the breeding behavior of two other North American *Elaphe* species in a paper by J. C. Gillingham (1979, *Copeia*, No. 2, pp 319-331). Gillingham divides corn snake courtship and mating into three phases: Tactile-chase (I), tactile-alignment (II), and intromission and coitus (III).

The tactile-chase phase begins when a male contacts a female with his snout and runs his chin forward along the back of the female. The female may respond by fleeing, and if so, the male will follow closely, continuing to try and maintain a position straddling along the back of the female. Late in this phase, the male corn snake may produce "caudocephalic waves", which are rippling motions made with his lower body against areas of the female's body in which he is in contact. These progress in a forward direction (hence the name) and may be accompanied by writhing motions of his trunk.

The second phase, tactile alignment, begins with the first tail-search copulatory attempt by the male and may continue to include caudocephalic waves. The copulatory attempts involve considerable twitching of the male's body and tail as he attempts to position his own vent underneath and align with the vent of the female in order to achieve intromission. Typically, only a few such copulatory attempts are required.

Phase III, intromission, occurs when the male everts one of his two spined hemipenes into the vent of the female. The considerable previous activity of the male will nearly cease once intromission is accomplished and often the only motion visible during mating itself is the slow waving of the tails of the animals. The total courtship time by the male is generally rather brief, probably lasting less time than the twenty minutes or so usually taken by intromission itself. Sometimes it can even be less than a minute. Unlike males of some snake species, including the related species *Elaphe obsoleta* (black rat snake group) and *Elaphe vulpina* (fox snake) that were studied by Gillingham, male corn snakes do not normally grasp the neck of the female in their jaws either during courtship or during mating, although I observed a single exception to this with a male corn snake that was the product of a cross between *E. g. guttata* and *E. g. emoryi* parents.

A telltale sign that mating has occurred is the presence of a small amount of a viscous yellowish fluid in the cage. This is characteristically left behind when a mating pair separates.

Individuals of both sexes may mate repeatedly during a single breeding season. In three instances, I have seen a female corn snake mate with two different males within a space of only about an hour and a half. I have yet to see copulations involving an individual male that were spaced closer than two days apart but I have been told that a pair of corn snakes that has just mated and is then separated for an hour or so may mate again if placed back together. This indicates that males will sometimes mate more than once per day.

Male Breeding Season Activity

During the height of the breeding season, adult male corn snakes are frequently very active, sometimes crawling around and trying to get out of their cages continuously. This is not searching for food, because, as has been stated, males have little or no appetite at this time. Undoubtedly, this restlessness has evolved to enhance their chances of finding mates. Males that spend the breeding season sitting in their burrows aren't likely to encounter females, while males out cruising around are obviously more likely to find them. However, activity does not necessarily assure that a particular male will actually be interested in mating. A highly active male may be quite uninterested in any female that may be introduced into his cage. This suggests that the internal mechanisms (presumably hormonal) that trigger activity and libido are not exactly the same. An animal's brain evidently may tell it to search without necessarily giving it a clue as to what it should be searching for.

Male Combat

Like males of many snake species, male corn snakes will physically battle one another during the breeding season. As larger males typically win such competitions, it is understandable that evolution has favored the attainment of large body size in male corn snakes, males of other snake species that have male combat (see Shine, R. 1979, *Oecologia* Vol. 33, pp. 269-277), and indeed, males of animal species in general where there is physical fighting for access to breeding females. Conversely, snake species such as garter snakes, where male combat is absent, typically have males that are smaller than the females. As an aside, it is perhaps worth noting that the norm of the animal kingdom is for females to be the larger sex since larger females can produce more offspring. This is typical of invertebrates and the "lower" vertebrates. Only the presence of male combat (which selects for large males) or parental care of offspring (which makes large broods infeasible) tends to favor smaller female size.

In male corn snakes, combat behavior appears to be initiated by a combination of chemical, visual, and tactile stimuli. Males can undoubtedly distinguish the scents of themselves both from reproductive females and from other males. A male in the breeding season can show keen interest (as manifested by considerable tongue flicking for at least a short period of time) if presented with a shed skin of another male and yet show no interest if presented with his own shed skin. This clearly demonstrates an ability to discriminate between his own scent and those of other males. Once in contact with one another, two males about to begin combat generally display a twitching behavior using their body which appears to help incite the conflict. Females also sometimes show this twitching behavior which perhaps could be very loosely interpreted as carrying the message "Don't mess with me!". Combatting truly begins once the males begin to twine around each other. Such twining is often very tight, especially toward the rear of the body. The males strain against one another while in this position with one male or the other occasionally flexing its body suddenly in a way that seems intended to overpower the second male. Males of about equal size may combat for a considerable period of time. Often, one male will decide he has had enough and break off the fight by dashing away. The victor may then chase the loser around and generally harass him if they are allowed to remain in the same cage together.

Even during the breeding season, one can generally keep more than one male per cage. Many males can be kept with one or two other males with minimal or no combat occurring. Even if fighting is sometimes seen between males in the same cage, it will often eventually give way to apparent truce. The most aggressive males on the other hand are probably best kept in cages without other males. They will not only participate in combats, but they will often stir

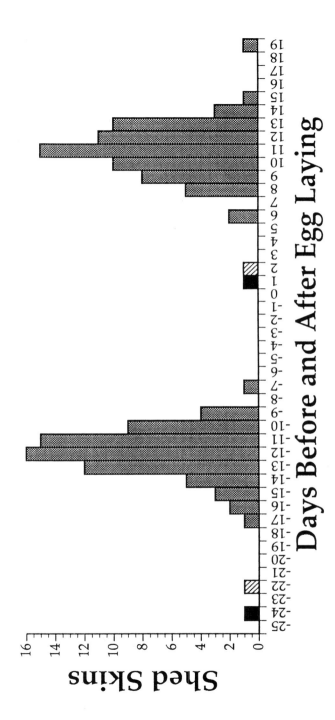

Figure 6. **Skin shedding before and after egg laying.** Day O represents the day that eggs are laid, and individual boxes represent shed skins that occur before (negative numbers) and after (positive numbers) egg laying. Striped boxes and black boxes indicate two instances of females that evidently were late in egg laying.

up less aggressive males into combats amongst themselves. Not infrequently, I will keep a small adult male in a cage with a much larger male. Such small males seem to have the sense (or at least quickly learn) not to pick fights with bigger males, but are not obviously inhibited as far as mating is concerned.

Pregnancy and Egg-Laying

In addition to the cessation of feeding that precedes egg-laying in corn snakes, there are other diagnostic signs of a female about to lay eggs. One, not surprisingly, is an increased girth in the abdominal area. This is usually, but not always, apparent. Another characteristic of pregnancy is the occurrence of a shed skin. A skin sloughing will almost always precede egg-laying and, as can be seen in Figure 6, the timing of this pre-lay shed is usually quite predictable, coming 10 to 14 days before eggs are laid. In what is probably an extreme exception to this, a female corn snake kept by Bill and Kathy Love usually lays when blue-eyed with its "pre-lay" shed. Yet another sign of a female about to lay eggs is a great increase in the animal's activity level, usually coming soon after the pre-egg-laying shed. This heightened activity is even more pronounced than that of males in the breeding season and reflects the female's search for the best place to lay her eggs. A day or two before laying, the female will generally settle down and stay in the place where she will wind up depositing her eggs.

With the type of set-up that I have, egg laying generally takes place in the soil underneath a hidebox or an inverted pie-tin. Only rarely are eggs laid within the drier confines of the inside of a hidebox, and with the occasional exception of a stray infertile egg, all laying occurs in some type of sheltered environment. In the unusual circumstance of laying occurring within a hide box, subsequent laying by another female within the same cage has been much more likely to also occur within the same hidebox. This indicates that the scent of eggs lingering in a location may be one of the cues that females use in choosing a place to lay eggs. One should be careful to ensure that a secluded and slightly moist area is available for a pregnant female to lay her eggs. Lack of a suitable place may lead to the female laying her eggs in the cage's water dish, an event which will quickly kill the embryos. Removing the water dish shortly before eggs are expected could assure that this won't happen.

Laying is usually completed over a period of less than a day. Exceptions occur sometimes when one or a few infertile eggs are laid early or late or when a female is egg bound and unable to lay all her eggs. Of 78 pregnancies that I have observed, three (4%) have produced egg bound animals. In one case, the eight infertile eggs were laid 13 to 21 days later. In a second case, 23 days after her initial egg-laying, an 18 gauge needle was put through the side of the

Two females that laid eggs the same day under a ceramic dish (lifted for photo). The smaller female laid 13 eggs and the larger one , 33 eggs.

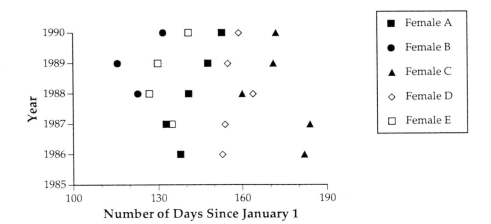

Figure 7. **Timing of the first clutch of eggs from several female corn snakes over a number of years.** January 1 is counted as Day 1. All females "came out" of hibernation at the same time at around day 60.

41

female, and the yolks of three unlaid eggs were removed. Two of the collapsed eggs were passed within a few hours, and the other passed within a day. In the third case, I was unable to remove much yolk using a needle and syringe at either 9 or 22 days after the initial laying, and the animal was taken to a veterinarian who palpated out one egg that had been next to the vent, administered antibiotics, and recommended force-feeding to allow the animal to regain some strength. Despite having been alert and fairly strong going in, this animal was dead six hours later.

One female corn snake that I have kept has never laid any eggs during her three adult years but has still shown behavior typical of pregnant females. She goes through the typical month long fast, sheds her skin, becomes very active like females soon to lay eggs, sheds her skin again, and resumes eating. I have not seen other any other female display a false pregnancy like this.

Individual females show different timing of their egg-laying with respect to the end of the hibernation period. Figure 7 shows the occurrence of the first clutch of the year for five females over a several year period. It is readily apparent from this that some females can be early layers, some can be late layers, and others can be intermediate in their timing. The time spread between the earliest and the latest seems to average about 50 days. Other females also appear to be generally predictable in the same fashion. These differences between females probably reflect adaptations to somewhat different environments from which the females (or their ancestors) originally came. The *E. guttata emoryi* female is the earliest layer, consistent with its observed pattern of having a short yearly eating period in suggesting that it originated in an area with a relatively short "growing season". Females that were particularly skinny coming out of hibernation can be delayed somewhat in the timing of their egg-laying based on the couple of cases that I have observed.

Size and Number of Eggs

The size of eggs also varies among different females. Figure 8 shows a graph of female body weight versus number of eggs laid that makes this very apparent. Two *E. guttata guttata* females show quite distinct and reproducible differences between themselves, and both of these animals produce smaller eggs than the *E. guttata emoryi* female. Also apparent from Figure 8 is the generally linear relationship between female body size and egg number. Typically, eggs from a given female seem to remain about the same size throughout most of the animal's life. Exceptions to this seem to often occur with the smallest adult females and with especially skinny females, both of which seem to lay somewhat smaller eggs. Egg shape appears to be able to vary more than egg size for a given female. In one year, a female may lay fairly

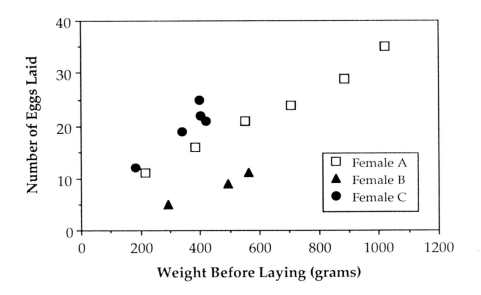

Figure 8. **Number of eggs laid in the first clutch of the year by three female corn snakes as a function of their body weight.** All clutches shown were fully fertile, or very nearly so. Female B is the *Elaphe guttata emoryi* female.

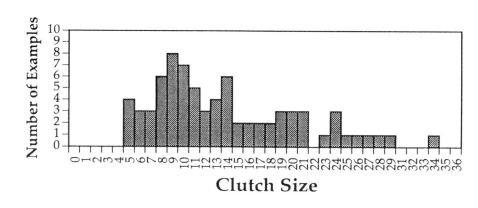

Figure 9. **Number of eggs laid per clutch (from the author's records).** Both fertile and infertile eggs are included.

round eggs, and in another year, they may be distinctly more elongate. Small females, perhaps not surprisingly, appear more likely to lay narrow, elongate eggs.

51 of the 78 clutches (66%) were from females laying their first (often only) clutch of the year, and the remaining 27 clutches were from females laying their second clutch of the year. As shown in Figure 9, the number of eggs in a clutch varies considerably. The mean clutch size (counting both fertile and infertile) produced by my females has been 15.3 for first clutches of the year and 11.0 for second clutches of the year (13.8 combined average). The smallest clutches I have seen were of five eggs (seen in four clutches), and the largest was 34 eggs. Ironically, these two extremes were produced by the same individual, the second clutch of her first year of reproducing and the first clutch from the past year prior to this writing. The most eggs in a single clutch that I have seen recorded for a corn snake is 40, 34 of which were fertile. Eggs that I have scored initially as infertile have constituted 19% of the 1078 eggs that I have seen laid (15% of first clutches and 28% of second clutches). For individual females, the percentage of infertile eggs (minimum three years of egg-laying) that I have observed ranges from 38% (19 of 50) to 0.4% (1 of 228). The yellowish infertile eggs do not adhere to one another in the manner of good eggs and invariably spoil within a few days.

If a second clutch occurs from a female, it is invariably smaller than her first clutch of the year. The second clutch will occur only about two months after the first and will be preceded by the normal pre-egglaying fast. Therefore, only a few weeks are available for regaining lost weight, a time period too short for full recovery. The partial weight recovery prior to the laying of a second clutch can be seen in Figure 5.

Recovery from Egg Laying

Laying eggs is a taxing experience for female corn snakes. One clutch of eggs will typically reduce a female's body weight by a third, and if a female double clutches in a particular year, her weight after laying the second clutch may be less than half of her peak weight earlier in the year. Delays in regaining this lost weight may jeopardize optimal reproduction the following year, and in extreme cases, may eventually lead to the death of the female. Particular care should therefore be taken to minimize the chances for problems after egg laying.

After laying their eggs, females almost always quickly go into another shedding cycle. As shown in Figure 6, egg-laying occurs midway between two sheddings spaced 20 to 30 days apart. In the two instances where a female shed only a couple of days after laying, the pre-lay shed was particularly early with

Two clutches with very different sized eggs. The large eggs (two fertile and one infertile) are from a Great Plains rat snake *(E.g. emoryi)* and the small eggs (20 smaller than average eggs) are from a corn snake *(Elaphe g. guttata.)* The females are about the same size.

respect to egg-laying. In one of these two instances, all eggs of the clutch were obviously infertile. In the second instance, all eggs of the clutch were scored as being good, but the eggs were delivered to another person, and I have no record of whether or not they hatched. The timing of the post-lay shed would seem to be linked to the timing of the pre-lay shed rather than to egg-laying itself. The post-lay shed may perhaps be useful in the wild as it probably increases the likelihood that the female will stay with her eggs until she sheds her skin, thereby offering some inadvertent protection to the new eggs.

Sometimes, after laying eggs, a female will be slow to recover her appetite. More typicallt however, females will eat voraciously soon after laying, often before their post-lay shed. I have in recent years become quite careful about feeding females after they have laid eggs. In their relatively emaciated states, they are often prone to developing regurgitation problems that can be severe enough to greatly limit the weight gain that should occur in the later part of the year. This can interfere with their ability to successfully lay eggs the following year. Though not all females appear to exhibit this problem, I now make the practice with all my females of restarting them eating with small sized meals. Animals that are particularly skinny or that have had a history of post-laying regurgitation problems will continue to be offered small meals at few day intervals until they regain a reasonable amount of weight. Females in better shape and with no history of such problems will get larger meals much sooner. Sometimes weight recovery will have been inadequate prior to when the animal would be normally hibernated. In most cases, such animals can still be hibernated without problems, though, as mentioned earlier, particularly skinny corn snakes tend to lose a much greater percentage of their body weight during hibernation than do other animals. To minimize the chances of starvation of very skinny animals, it may at times be desirable to shorten or eliminate the hibernation period.

Skinny female corn snakes may still lay eggs in the breeding season. This is not necessarily desirable as it can leave the female in a very emaciated state. It would sometimes seem preferable to have a female avoid egg-laying in a given year to allow her more time to regain weight. Unfortunately, keeping thin females apart from males during the breeding season will not reliably prevent egg-laying. The eggs laid will simply be sterile.

Incubation and Hatching of Eggs

Fertile corn snake eggs will generally adhere tightly to one another, and often all the eggs of a clutch will be stuck together in a single clump. Eggs that are stuck together can be carefully pulled apart with some difficulty, but it is not recommended to do so. When a female has finished laying her eggs, I transfer them into a lidded plastic shoe box that is 50-70% filled with moist vermiculite (some breeders use sphagnum moss instead). I use new vermiculite each year to eliminate the chance of carrying over potentially deleterious fungi from used vermiculite. The freshly laid eggs are placed on the surface of the vermiculite so they can be readily observed. The appropriate amount of water to have present in the vermiculite is the minimum amount necessary that allows the eggs to be turgid or no more than slightly indented. 1 volume of water for 10-15 volumes of vermiculite is a good place to start. Additional small amounts of water may need to be added as evaporation occurs. Many plastic shoe boxes have sufficiently loose lids that additional holes for aeration are unnecessary. If you choose to make air holes, be sure they are smaller than 1/8" (3 mm) in diameter to prevent hatchlings from escaping.

A good temperature range for incubating corn snake eggs is 80°-85° F (27°-30° C), although temperature variation between 70° F and 90 F (21°-32° C) can certainly be tolerated. The fairly warm temperatures of egg incubation will often require external heating. This can be provided by commercial or home-made incubators or by something as simple as a heating pad. Should you choose to use a heating pad, monitor the temperature carefully, as they can very easily fatally overheat the eggs. However you heat eggs, be sure to

Seven clutches of eggs in shoe boxes with moistened vermiculite (uncovered for photo).

take into account the potential for temperature rises due to hot weather. Aim for not letting eggs get hotter than 90° F (32° C) and remember that too cool is better than too hot. I incubate my eggs in the heated shelves that house my hatchling and young snakes, an arrangement which, while convenient, is probably not optimal as it creates some minor problems for incubating eggs. An individual shelf is heated with heat-tape which sits underneath a sheet of thin aluminum wide enough to disperse heat to about 2/3 of the box. This creates warmer and cooler zones useful for baby snakes to choose from but which leads to condensation of water at the cool end of the box, on the underside of the lid, and sometimes on the underside of eggs. This makes it important to occasionally stir up the vermiculite to redistribute the moisture in the box. Eggs should not be allowed to become wet. Wet areas can quickly be subject to fungal attack and should be scrupulously avoided. This may require frequently checking the bottoms of eggs that are heated from underneath. Slowly collapsing eggs are either kept conditions that are too dry or they do not contain a living embryo. If they are still alive they should begin to expand within a few days if covered with more moist vermiculite. A modest amount of indenting of eggs is normal in the days immediately prior to hatching.

A minority of eggs that appear more or less good upon laying also spoil during the course of incubation, usually very early on. Some clutches of eggs are definitely more prone to this than others. One potential cause of this may be infertility. Eggs that look fairly good or even perfectly good can still sometimes be infertile and can go a full term of incubation without necessarily spoiling. Perhaps infertility is responsible for why some eggs look good for a while, but then rather quickly collapse and die.

Another potential contribution to the early demise of eggs involves problems with the shell. In a few instances, clutches have had many eggs with many translucent patches where deposition of the shell was faulty. These eggs seem more prone to spoiling in spite of being fertile. Rarely, eggs will even develop small holes in their surfaces and begin to ooze fluid. Such holes promote microbial growth (if indeed they are not caused by microbial growth in the first place) and may lead to the death of the embryo, though one egg survived more than two weeks of on and off leaking to hatch successfully. Of all eggs initially scored as being good, some 80-85% have hatched. A minority of clutches account for a majority of non-hatching eggs and many clutches show 100% hatching.

The time period between the laying of eggs and their subsequent hatching varies depending upon the temperature. The first year I had eggs, they were all kept without any outside heat source. An autumn clutch essentially remained at room temperature ($\sim 21°$ C) for their entire incubation and hatched 96-100 days after being laid. Only four of the eight eggs of this clutch hatched, and these babies were very small, having not absorbed much of their yolk sacs which remained within their eggs. One of the babies died within a day of hatching. The four eggs that did not hatch contained dead, but fully developed babies that were presumably too weak to emerge from their eggs. Two other clutches laid earlier in the summer of that same year and exposed to a variable but somewhat higher average room temperature hatched 93-102 days and 84-89 days after being laid. The eggs taking 84-89 days came from the same female as the eggs described above. The babies from these clutches developed and hatched without problems. In subsequent years, I have kept eggs in boxes with vermiculite that are heated from below to temperatures that are generally between 82° F and 90° F (28°-32° C). Under these conditions hatching begins to occur from 52 to 60 days after laying. Those eggs of a clutch that are nearer the warm end of the egg box tend to hatch sooner than those toward the cooler end. This was especially apparent in one clutch laid in a long string where the eggs hatched in rough order from the warm end down to the cool end. I have observed that the hatching of a clutch of eggs is generally spread out over several days and has lasted as long as eight days, though the temperature gradient present in my incubation boxes undoubtedly lengthens the spread of hatching time. Eggs from all of my different females hatch in about the same length of time when temperatures of incubation are equivalent. More controlled conditions of egg incubation would be needed to detect possible small differences between females if they are present.

Hatching begins with the baby using its egg tooth to slice one or more small slits through the egg shell. The slits invariably occur on the top side of the egg. When handling eggs for any reason, I always make sure to keep the same side face up to avoid any potential for changed orientation of the egg to hamper normal development of the embryo. Emerging from the top of the egg can present a problem for babies in eggs stuck directly underneath another egg. In such cases, it may be advisable to gently detach any such bottom eggs around the time when the eggs are expected to hatch. After slitting open a hole in its egg, a hatchling corn snake will remain for about a day in its shell with only its head sticking out before fully emerging. Allow hatchlings to emerge on their own. Any egg that seems good but that has not slit despite all its neighboring eggs having opened will probably contain either a dead fetus or an animal that may be too weak to cut through the shell. Some deaths of full term fetuses can be prevented if eggs that seem late in hatching are carefully slit open on their top surface with a razor blade. This will ensure that weaker babies are at least able to get through the shell.

Of the 1000 or so corn snake eggs that I have hatched to date, a single one contained a pair of twins.

Tease-feeding by inciting a hatchling corn snake to strike at a pre-killed "pink" mouse can be a useful technique for getting a reluctant feeder to begin feeding. Photo by Bill Love.

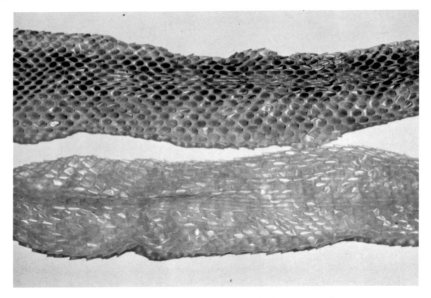

The shed skins from normal (top) and amelanistic corn snakes.

Skin Shedding

Like other snakes, corn snakes periodically shed their skins. The shedding cycle first becomes noticeable when the snake's normal coloration starts becoming rather dull and when the eyes cloud over and appear blue. After a few days, the eyes clear again, and within a few days after that, the snake will shed its skin. The entire process takes one to two weeks in adults and somewhat less time in young corn snakes. As in other snakes, shedding in corn snakes begins with the animal rubbing its nose to loosen the skin above and below its mouth, then peeling off the skin inside out, usually in a single piece. The blotched pattern of the skin is typically visible in a molted skin as a faint brownish pattern. In contrast, the molted skins of amelanistic corn snakes lack this brownish coloration.

Although a dried shed skin weighs only about half of one percent of the weight of the animal from which it came, it is associated with a 2.5-3% weight loss. One shed skin thus appears to cause as much weight loss as two to three months of winter fasting. The additional weight loss beyond the weight of the dried skin may stem partly from water lost with the skin when it is shed, but probably mostly comes from the metabolic cost of having to synthesize a new skin layer.

The annual frequency of shed skins for juvenile and adult corn snakes is shown in Figure 10. During their first full calendar year, young corn snakes that I have kept have shed their skins seven to thirteen times, typically at quite regular intervals. Even babies that are growing at a relatively modest rate can be among those showing the greatest number of sheds. This apparent paradox may be due to the fact that slower growing individuals remain in the warmer "baby boxes" longer than most of the faster growing individuals that I have kept. Adults of both sexes typically shed six to eight times per year. The instances of fewer yearly totals appear to be due either to errors in record keeping (not recording some sheds) or to circumstances where the individual (typically female) actually lost weight during the year. Growth rate appears to make no difference in the shedding frequency of adults. Adults that show no net weight gain during the year shed just as often as adults that are doubling in weight during the course of the year. It should be noted, however, that none of my adults exceed eight or nine years of age. The shedding frequencies of old animals may turn out to be lower. Additionally, I've been told that snakes with fresh skin wounds will go through a series of closely spaced sheds.

Among hibernated adult corn snakes, shedding generally does not occur (or occurs once) during the three month hibernation period. As already mentioned, one shed occurs a month or so after the end of the hibernation period

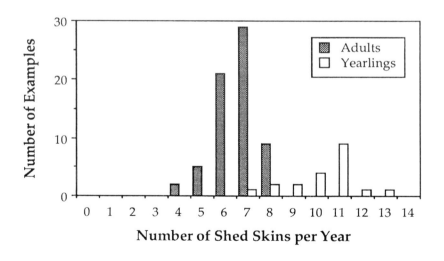

Figure 10. **Frequency of skin shedding in juvenile and adult corn snakes.** The yearly period measured begins January 1.

51

in both sexes and sheds occur both soon before and soon after egg laying in females. The shedding pattern over several years of an adult female is shown in Figure 11A. The tightly spaced sheds occurring before and after egg-laying readily stand out.

A surprising result of plotting the occurrences of shed skins came with some of the adult males. Three of the five adult males that I have kept for at least four years, as well as other males I have had for shorter periods, all show very similar shedding patterns every year. The most regular case is shown in Figure 11B which plots the occurrence of shedding for one male over a number of years. This animal has been found to shed seven times each year with even the spacing between sheds being generally conserved from year to year. Curiously, both for this male and for most other males that I have, the time period between the second and third sheds of the year is usually the shortest of any interval between shed skins. The shortest period between shed skins that I have seen for any corn snake, juvenile or adult (16 days), came between the second and third sheds of the year for a five year old male. The short period between the second and third sheds can be true even when no eating occurs during this period (as was the case for the 16 day period mentioned above). Conceivably, the hormonal mechanism that produces the short period between the second and third sheds of females (pre and post-lay sheds) may also be active in many males.

A container of moist peat moss will incite a gravid female to lay her eggs. It will also facilitate shedding.

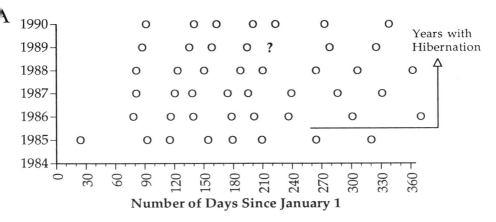

Figure 11A. **Shedding records of adult corn snakes over a several year period. Numbering of days begins with January 1.** The first year that my adults were hibernated was 1986. A. Shedding record of a female corn snake. The question mark indicates the possible timing of a post-egglaying shed for which I have no record. Conceivably, this shed may have been skipped on this occasion.

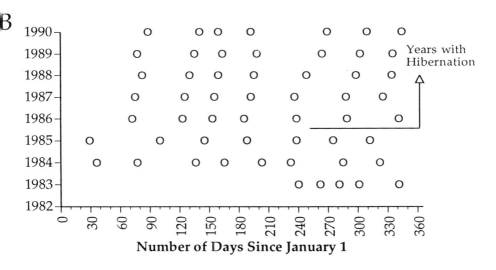

Figure 11B. **Shedding record of a male corn snake with a particularly regular shedding pattern.**

Diseases and Disorders

Introduction

Corn snakes, particularly if captive-raised from hatchlings, are among the easiest to keep and least disease prone of snakes that are maintained in captivity. Nonetheless, they are potentially subject to a variety of maladies, many of which can be treated successfully. This section describes some of the more common health problems seen with corn snakes and describes courses of action that the snake keeper, or in some cases, a veterinarian, can follow to prevent or treat the problems.

Shedding problems

Corn snakes should shed their skins without difficulty with the shed skin generally coming off as a single piece. Problems with shedding may arise if a cage has too little humidity or if a snake is particularly late in trying to start the removal process. Under such circumstances, the skin that is due to come off becomes difficult to separate from the underlying skin and shedding may be incomplete or may result in many torn pieces. Soaking a snake in water for awhile, or leaving a snake overnight in a damp cloth sack with damp moss in it, can make it easier for either the snake or the keeper to peel off the remaining skin. It is preferable to remove all of an old skin if at all possible. For example, if old skin is left on the very tip of the tail, it may cause the tail tip to die and eventually fall off. While this appears not to be harmful to the snake, it can be avoided if shed skins are completely removed from the tail. Great care should be taken if one tries to remove adhering spectacles (the scales covering the eyes of snakes). For many small pieces of adhering skin, it may be best to simply wait. These remaining bits will come off when the snake sheds the next time. If a snake fails to shed any of its skin after having been through a blue-eyed period, the subsequent shed may remove two old layers together.

I've been told that too much humidity can also potentially lead to shedding problems. If this is suspected, try using a cage with better ventilation.

Snake Mites

The best defense against these tiny blood-sucking parasites is prevention of ever having them come into your collection. Always quarantine new snakes to ensure that they do not transmit mites to the rest of your collection. However, should your corn snake ever become infested with mites, they can, with some difficulty, be effectively eliminated. Left untreated, they potentially can kill snakes.

The first step in dealing with snake mites is detecting them. Mites are visible as tiny (~1 mm), dark, round bugs that attach themselves between scales and around the eyes. They may well be seen crawling about on the snake, in the cage, or on your hands after handling an infested snake. Mite feces, visible as fine white flecks may also be seen. Once a mite infestation becomes severe, it will be difficult to overlook, however, it is obviously best to discover it early. Looking at the inside of a shed skin is an excellent way of checking for mites, because the mites will be peeled off along with the skin. Shedding, if it occurs in one piece, will rid the snake of mites but of course will not prevent re-infestation from mites still in the cage.

Treatment of a mite infestation must deal with both the snake and the snake's cage and perhaps the area immediately surrounding the cage as well. The snake can be removed from the infested cage and placed for a few hours in an escape-proof cage with enough water in it to just submerse the snake. This will wash off and drown many of the mites. Meanwhile, the cage substrate should be discarded, any cage items thoroughly scrubbed and cleaned, and the cage itself should be wiped both inside and out with a 3% bleach solution. The snake can then be placed back in the cage. At this point, a 1" by 2" section of Vapona pest strip (active ingredient: 2.2 dichlorovinyl dimethyl phosphate) should be placed inside a perforated container inside the cage. The vapor should be able to get out without the snake being able to come in contact with the pest strip. Strips that have turned green (they are normally yellow) will not be effective. Leave the container with the Vapona strip in the cage for 24 hours, then check the cage bottom for live mites. If live mites are still present, wait another 24 hours. Thoroughly wipe the outside of the cage again to remove any mites that may have crawled out. Repeat the Vapona treatment again after ten days.

Rubbed Noses

A fairly frequent injury among some snake species is a damaged nose caused by incessant rubbing on the walls or top of a cage in attempts to get out of a cage. Although corn snakes, in general, do not appear to be very prone to severe nose-rubbing problems, I have seen a few juveniles that were kept in plastic shoe boxes without a shelter develop quite swollen noses from rubbing. The problem did not persist once the animals were moved into more spacious cages containing shelters.

Egg-binding

Female corn snakes are sometimes unable to lay their entire clutch of eggs. Such individuals are referred to as being egg-bound and may require prompt treatment in order to survive. If a female still has lumps in her from unlaid eggs for more than a day after having laid the rest of the clutch, it may well be that she will never be able to lay them on her own without intervention. A veterinarian with experience treating reptiles may be able to remove the remaining eggs either by administering a hormone to induce labor, by palpation, or by surgery. An alternate means that can be effective uses a needle and syringe to drain some of the contents out of the eggs and make them easier for the animal to pass on her own. This technique is best carried out by two people. The sites of needle insertion should be wiped with alcohol prior to the actual insertions. A large (18 or 20 gauge works well) sterile needle, attached to a 10 cc syringe is inserted between scales mid-way up the side of the female directly into the middle of an unlaid egg. The syringe is then used to suck up as much of the egg contents as possible. More than one try per egg may be needed. Often, unlaid eggs can be substantially reduced in size by this and will be passed as collapsed shells within a day by the female. If done correctly, the risk of infection from this technique appears to be low. Unfortunately, not all eggs have an appreciable level of fluid in them that can be removed by this technique. To have the best chance of being effective, this technique should be done fairly soon after any other eggs have been laid. After one to three weeks have passed, the unlaid eggs are likely to solidify and become impossible to aspirate with a needle. Eggs very near the vent can sometimes be aspirated by passing the needle directly through the cloacal opening.

Internal Parasites

Wild-collected corn snakes may harbor nematode worms and/or tapeworms. If a wild-collected corn snake eats regularly, has more or less normal looking stools (not runny or discolored) yet fails to gain weight then a stool check should be performed by a veterinarian to determine the presence of internal parasites. Corn snakes may also be infected with protozoan parasites such as amoebas, trichomonads or coccidia. The following are parasiticides commonly used in treating snakes:

For treatment of nematodes:

Levamisole hydrochloride: 10 mg/kg. Administered orally or can be injected intraperitoneally. Repeat once in two weeks.
Thiabendazole: 75 mg/kg, administered orally. Repeat once in two weeks.
Fenbendazole: 75 mg/kg, administered orally. Repeat once in two weeks.

For treatment of tapeworms (cestodes):
Praziquantel: 5-8 mg/kg, administered orally. Repeat once in two weeks.

For treatment of amebas and trichomonads:
Metronidazole: 100 mg/kg, administered orally. Repeat once in two weeks.

For treatment of coccidia:
Sulfamethazine: 75 mg/kg, given orally on first day, then 45 mg/kg administered daily for five days.

The above dosages are adopted from R. S. Funk and S. L. Barten, 1987, "Fecal analysis workshop; Table 1" in 10th and 11th International Herpetological Symposium on Captive Propagation and Husbandry, p. 166.

Respiratory problems
Relative to many species of snakes, corn snakes are quite resistant to respiratory infections but individuals exposed to cool temperatures for prolonged periods of time, and animals exposed to other diseased animals will be more susceptible. Early symptoms may include a slight wheezing and the presence of bubbly mucus inside the mouth and sometimes alongside the mouth. Snakes with respiratory infections are often more listless and may eventually stop feeding. As the disease progresses, a snake will gape and occasionally forcibly exhale air. Once the disease has progressed to this stage, a snake will die if the disease is left untreated. In the early stages, the best course of treatment is to keep the snake warmer round the clock at temperatures of 85°-88° F (24°-26° C). If no signs of improvement are visible within a week or if the condition worsens, a veterinarian should be consulted for the administration of injectable antibiotics such as Amikacin.

Gastroenteritis
The typical symptoms of enteritis may include regurgitation, diarrhea, smelly stools, discolored stools, blood in the stools, loss of appetite, loss of weight and dehydration. If untreated, gastroenteritis is often fatal. The only treatment is to have stool checks and cultures performed by a qualified veterinarian to determine the best course of action. With treatment, prognosis is good.

Keeping snakes at temperatures that are too cool and/or under unsanitary conditions increases susceptibility to this disorder. Cooling down animals for the winter hibernation before they have fully digested their last meals can be a cause of gastroenteritis. Gastroenteritis is more prevalent in wild-collected animals sold in the pet trade, than in captive-bred and raised individuals.

Infectious Stomatitis (Mouth rot)

Mouth rot is a bacterial infection of the gums of snakes. Early symptoms of mouth rot consist of the presence of whitish caseous matter inside and along the rim of the mouth. Sometimes it is first noticed when a snake isn't able to close its mouth properly or when a small amount of crusty matter is present along one side of the rim of the mouth. The disease can be passed to other snakes and afflicted animals should therefore be quarantined. Treatment of the disease in snakes involves gently wiping off as much encrusted matter as possible and applying a 3 % hydrogen peroxide solution followed by Betadine (povidone-iodine). This treatment should be carried out each day until the infection has cleared, usually within a couple of weeks. Serious infections are best treated with antibiotics administered by a veterinarian.

Thankfully, mouthrot seems to be quite uncommon among corn snakes, especially captive-raised ones.

About the Author

Mike McEachern was born in Wyandotte, Michigan in 1958. His interest in snakes and other animals began in childhood and has remained with him ever since. He has kept reptiles, primarily snakes, continuously since 1973 and began keeping corn snakes in 1983. Currently, 30 corn snakes comprise his entire animal collection.

Professionally, Mike works as a molecular biologist studying bacteria and yeasts. He received a B. S. in biology from the University of Michigan in 1980 and a Ph. D. in biology from the University of California at San Diego in 1987. He has done post-doctoral work at Scripps Clinic and Research Foundation in La Jolla, California and, at the time of this publication, is continuing post-doctoral work at the University of California at San Francisco. This book is his first publication dealing with reptiles.

Acknowledgements: The author would like to thank Philippe de Vosjoli, Bill & Kathy Love, Rich Zuchowski, and Dorothy DeLisle for their help in the preparation of this book. I would also like to thank Denise Wyborski for help with the photography.

AVAILABLE AUGUST 1991

The companion book to
Keeping and Breeding Corn Snakes
by Michael J. McEachern

"A Color Guide to Corn Snakes Captive-bred in the United States"
By Michael J. McEachern

- A genetics primer on corn snakes.

- Background information on all morphs currently bred in the United States.

- Thirty (30) color photographs illustrating corn snakes morphs.

This is the professional reference book that herpetoculturists have been waiting for. Soon available through local pet stores and book dealers. Published by Advanced Vivarium Systems.